IMAGES
of America

CALAIS

The *Nexus*, carved from local red granite in 2014 by sculptor Miles Chapin, symbolizes the importance of relationships and connections. It stands in Triangle Park, in front of the Calais Free Library. (Author's collection.)

IMAGES
of America

CALAIS

Lura Jackson with
the St. Croix Historical Society
Foreword by Al Churchill

ARCADIA
PUBLISHING

Published by Arcadia Publishing
Charleston, South Carolina

Printed in the United States of America

Library of Congress Control Number: 2020930354

For all general information, please contact Arcadia Publishing:
Telephone 843-853-2070
Fax 843-853-0044
E-mail sales@arcadiapublishing.com
For customer service and orders:
Toll-Free 1-888-313-2665

Visit us on the Internet at www.arcadiapublishing.com

To John, for exemplifying the gift of existence; to Da, for embracing our shared lives together; and to the people of Calais, for the future

CONTENTS

FOREWORD

Human habitation in the St. Croix Valley began between 10,000 and 14,000 years ago with the arrival of the first Native Americans. These progenitors of today's Passamaquoddy spent the spring and summer months along the area's resource-rich shores fishing for pollock, hunting seals, and harvesting clams and other shellfish. The Passamaquoddy were good stewards of the land, never wasteful or taking game unless required for the survival of the tribe.

The first Europeans to arrive were the French, who attempted to establish a settlement in 1604 at St. Croix Island, seven miles below what is now Calais. This was the first European settlement in North America north of St. Augustine, Florida. After a year, the French abandoned the settlement but not the valley, continuing to trade with the Passamaquoddy for the next 100 years until the area became central to the struggle for dominance between France and England, a contest eventually won by the English.

By the late 1700s, the rich fishing grounds and virgin forests began to attract a large number of English settlers. In the beginning, life was a struggle, but by the 1830s, lumber was in high demand in the large cities to the west, and the hinterlands of the St. Croix Valley had a seemingly unlimited supply. Shipbuilding and lumber exports became the lifeblood of the valley, and huge fortunes were made and sometimes lost.

Deforestation, along with the end of the age of sail, resulted in severe economic problems for the area. However, immigrants found the valley very welcoming, and they began to arrive in large numbers in the late 1800s, establishing businesses, and immigrant labor built the railroads, the paper mill, and the streetcar and water systems. Many of the immigrant laborers remained to work in the mills and factories. From the late 1800s until the 1960s, Calais thrived as a commercial center for a large geographical area.

Much has changed in the last couple of decades, as it has in all geographically isolated communities. Urban areas have attracted many of our young people, and local businesses find it difficult to compete with big box stores and Amazon. Nonetheless, the St. Croix Valley remains a very attractive area with a beautiful river, an industrious population, and a good deal of hope that its future is bright.

—Al Churchill

ACKNOWLEDGMENTS

Grateful thanks to the officers and members of the St. Croix Historical Society who have labored to collect and preserve the history of the valley throughout the decades. The author also extends personal thanks to Al Churchill for his willingness to review this manuscript and provide guidance on key points.

Unless otherwise noted, all images in this book appear courtesy of the St. Croix Historical Society.

INTRODUCTION

How can you tell the story of a place? No living person remembers the St. Croix Valley when it was new, a scar freshly cut into granite bedrock by the massive weight of receding ice. Nor do firsthand records exist of the earliest humans who made their way into the rugged landscape, following the great game herds feasting on the fields of sweet young vegetation.

But humans were here, and the relationship between Calais and humanity was being interwoven long before it was incorporated as a municipality. These are the stories that have been handed down between the generations living here, first between the indigenous peoples—"95 percent of the history of the valley is Passamaquoddy," as Al Churchill, president of the St. Croix Historical Society, has said—and then between the non-natives that came to call Calais home.

This book is an archive of stories told one at a time and shared between hundreds of people. Most of it exists because the facts were written down at some point; all of it exists because those seeing it and hearing it saw the value in maintaining a record of humanity's ongoing activities that define daily modern life in momentous ways. The present, after all, is a collection of the layers of history we exist with—and the history we are able to remember.

Located in the far northeast, Calais is among the most easterly places in the United States. Its long history is characterized by the unshakable truths of this geographic location: a relentless winter that often spans half the year, easy access to the coast and subsequently all ports in the world, and a massive hardwood and pine forest spanning as far inland as even the most intrepid explorer could determine.

Its very remoteness is what made the St. Croix Valley attractive to early American settlers at first. This was the wild northern frontier—far from the governing bodies in Massachusetts, free from religious establishments and the threat of persecution, and open to the possibility of new expansion. After going almost as far as they could through the eastern forests, those first settlers found the St. Croix River to be the perfect location for a bright and promising future.

The small groups of settlers met and were often guided by the Passamaquoddy as they made their way through the rugged, maze-like landscape. The Passamaquoddy were generally welcoming of the Europeans they encountered, only rising to conflict when their lands or their people were taken or destroyed, a pattern employed most often by the English. When possible, the preference between both settlers and natives was to establish friendly relations—as to be at war in such a far-removed and challenging place was tantamount to self-destruction.

As such, the spirit of welcoming and cooperation was born from necessity, settling in to the valley as it grew from being the ancestral home of traveling family bands of Passamaquoddy to a burgeoning river port. The first settlers of European descent found Calais to be an ideal location for establishing a lumber trade, and they were soon joined by hundreds more seeking to build their lives in the New World around the foresting industry.

From that simple equation, the history of modern Calais took root. Families freely settled on both sides of the river; later they had to determine whether they wanted to continue to exist on the Calais side—claimed by the United States—or the St. Stephen side—the territory of England, or what would become Canada.

For the Passamaquoddy people caught in between, the decision was unthinkable. The St. Croix River was not a border but a connection; it was not meant to divide but to unite. Large Passamaquoddy groups existed on both sides of the river; their long history saw them moving without regard to invisible boundaries as the needs of the season required. While the Passamaquoddy were able to remain present in the valley—avoiding the fate of native tribes who are now extinct—the perspective of the river and what it represents was permanently altered when the valley became an industrialized international border.

The history that emerged from the now-conjoined existence of the St. Croix Valley, the Passamaquoddy, and the settlers is unlike any other in the world. At the same time, it is a story familiar to any student of the postcolonial era in the United States. Devastation wrought the natives as their lands were seized; early industry thrived and the settlement boomed; growth slowed as the industrial era became dominated by larger, more powerful cities; and a modern era characterized by the remnants of the past and the carefully watered seeds of the hopeful future. Considered broadly, this is the story of America, unfolding in various ways in settlement after settlement across the country's wide expanse.

Looked at in detail, however, the story of Calais is indeed unique. Here was the first Christmas celebrated north of Virginia and the first newspaper in North America. It was this place in which the earliest field recordings in the world—taken using Thomas Edison's wax cylinder machine by a young anthropologist seeking to preserve what he recognized as the then-precarious culture of the Passamaquoddy—were made. It was Calais that served as a link for the determination of longitude by telegraph on December 16, 1866, thus removing the need for time and place to be established by chronometers carried on ships during transatlantic voyages. Though remote and fairly small for a city, Calais has played pivotal roles in the history of the state, the nation, and the world.

Despite its occasionally prominent history, the people of the St. Croix Valley are not characteristically prideful. The landscape remains as unforgiving as it was when settlers first arrived, and time to bask in the glory of yesteryear is short when preparations for next winter are seemingly always at hand. Reserved and hardworking, those living in Calais and the surrounding areas famously exemplify the Down Easter mentality of stoic independence mixed with a quick readiness to help a neighbor in need.

Many families can count backward through the generations to find their first relatives to arrive in Down East Maine. Being the descendants of nine generations lends an unmitigated clout to residents who call the valley home, and those who are "from away" will bear that distinction no matter how long they reside in Calais. To be from this place is to be born of its land and history; to have eaten from the soil, drunk the water, and breathed the air for all of one's existence and well beyond. It means to have experienced and survived winter after winter, watching the snow pack climb higher and higher as the fuel dwindles. It means to have known the bliss of spring in the valley and to have shared in that relief with all of one's family, friends, and neighbors.

To be frank, no settler of purely European descent can come close to realizing the full truth of the ancestral relationship with place as the Passamaquoddy. The rich myths recounting how the Passamaquoddy came to be in this land are extensive and include the very creation of their people from the trees they continue to harvest for basketmaking. Over time, this understanding of interconnection with the land was gravely endangered as European nations, the State of Maine, and then the United States itself as governing powers labored to suppress and ultimately annihilate native culture. Thankfully, this push toward cultural genocide has lessened, and the Passamaquoddy today are able to honor at least some of the traditions that have enabled their people to thrive in the St. Croix Valley for thousands of years.

Some reparations have been made to remedy the loss of the Passamaquoddy. At the federal level, Pres. Jimmy Carter signed the Indian Land Claims Act in 1980, resulting in more than $81 million being given to the tribes of Maine. On the part of the state, the Maine Wabanaki–State

Child Welfare Truth and Reconciliation Commission was launched in 2013, being the first of its kind in the world. The commission had a goal of determining the extent of the abuse and loss experienced during the forced cultural assimilation of the past centuries, and it continues to serve as the bedrock for tribal relations moving forward.

In Calais itself, a modern community has emerged after a century of slow decline. Today's residents are native and foreign-born, local and from away. Passamaquoddy is taught in the high school to natives and non-natives alike. Overseas investors and residents make their way to the remote area to explore its potential and make use of its quiet lifestyle. Canadian shoppers cross the bridges frequently to take advantage of the United States market and purchase goods that would otherwise be harder to procure. Americans from distant states establish their lives here, drawn by work with the US Border Patrol or the medical industry. The community of Calais continues to evolve, and so too does its story.

Like any physical record of history, this book is challenged in the sense that it is of limited space. The thousands of people that have lived in Calais have done so energetically for as long as it has been established, and capturing all of these exploits in such a format is simply not possible. As such, the history presented in photographs here is but a snapshot taken at different times as the full picture steadily unfolds in the lives happening around it. May this book serve as an open window to the past and the future of the city still gleaming on the banks of the St. Croix.

One

PREHISTORY TO EUROPEAN CONTACT

PASSAMAQUODDY PEOPLE TO 1604 FRENCH SETTLEMENT

The earliest humans to arrive in the St. Croix Valley followed the Laurentide Ice Sheet as it retreated more than 11,000 years ago. Their existence was shaped by the land they inhabited; it became an intrinsic part of their daily lives and their enduring cultural story.

The long, frigid winters of the newly uncovered landscape were not easily overcome, but, aided by the knowledge and tools carried with them during their migration across the Great Plains, these first humans readily adapted. Using Clovis-point weapons, they hunted caribou, giant beavers, mammoths, and mastodons, utilizing all parts of their prey to fullest effect.

Key to those living in the valley was the river they knew as Skutik. Reaching far inland to myriad lakes, fed by numerous tributaries, and extending to the bountiful coast, the river was a means of vital connection. In the summer, the people traveled to the mouth of the river to stay at Sipayik, a peninsula extending into the frigid ocean. There, they harvested abundant shellfish, hunted porpoises and whales, and caught ample fish. Their proclivity for a particular fish granted them their name: Pestomuhkatiyik (Passamaquoddy), or "people of the pollock spearing place."

In the fall, the Passamaquoddy left the coast to follow caribou and moose during their rutting season. The compulsion to procreate reliably made such game more active in the daylight, making them easy prey for savvy hunters.

In the winter, the Passamaquoddy retreated up the river to a lakeside village, Motahkomikuk. There, they found much-needed shelter from the fierce ocean winds and sustenance in the form of large game. The extended evenings were met in expertly made teepees warmed with steady fires as elders shared stories of times long past and the spiritual and energetic forces at play in and around the village.

In the spring, the Passamaquoddy gathered at the waterfalls along the river for the annual running of the salmon. Their campsites on the warming ground were a site of joyous feasting on the richly nutritious fish flesh.

In this fashion, the Passamaquoddy existed for thousands of years in and around the area that would later become known as Calais.

Upon arriving in the St. Croix Valley, the first humans found it to be teeming with wildlife. As the glacier continued to recede, mammals like the white-tailed deer spread throughout the dense forests. The Passamaquoddy hunted the deer for food and utilized all parts of the animal for everything from clothing to fishnets to thrive in the cold climate.

Near the coast, a large marsh the Passamaquoddy called Maguerrowock was easily navigable by birchbark canoes. The name translates to "land of the caribou," as it was there that a great herd of marsh caribou made its home in the winter months. The caribou was an important source of food to the Passamaquoddy.

The artery of the St. Croix Valley, which enabled the Passamaquoddy to travel freely between their winter and summer villages and well beyond, was the Skutik, a river 71 miles in length. Lined with shallow waters meeting the coast that receded regularly during the area's 20-foot tides, the river was easily accessible and filled with food. The Passamaquoddy had several sites along the Skutik that served as shellfish gathering locations, some of which have been identified in modern times by the presence of shell middens. Beyond the mudflats, the Skutik held the fresh memory of being carved out by the receding ice sheet, signified by the exposed granite bedrock on its shores. Growing from the fertile soil along the banks are white birch trees. According to Passamaquoddy tradition, birch trees are among the sacred gifts provided by the Creator, Glooskap, enabling them to build canoes, shelters, containers, traps, and many other items helpful for survival.

While in its more modern incarnation, this view of the Skutik clearly shows the long stretches of shoreline that can commonly be seen as the tides recede, thus exposing the food-rich intertidal zone. Sheltering coves are abundant along its banks, allowing travelers to seek refuge during high winds or the onset of darkness.

In places along the Skutik, its narrowing banks produce high rapids that are safely navigated by only the most skilled canoeists. To avoid the potential dangers of paddling through such unruly waters, the Passamaquoddy would carefully plan their trips along the river to sync with the times when the currents were slowest.

Chief Neptune   Chief Tomah of Peter Dana Point, Princeton Me.

The Passamaquoddy people appointed chiefs, called *sakom*, to lead their villages in decisions ranging from disputes with neighboring groups to trade and resource sharing. These two men, Chief Neptune and Sabattis Tomah, are excellent representatives of what tribal leaders would have appeared and functioned as. The Neptunes provided a long line of chiefs to the tribe, while Sabattis Tomah (1873–1954) was a keeper of ceremonial songs, medicinal plants, and indigenous knowledge who strove to preserve the culture of his people. They are seen here at what is now known as Peter Dana Point, near the winter village Motahkomikuk. Records of the chief-making ceremony of the Passamaquoddy are still in existence and outline the procedure. Chiefs tended to live long lives unless beset by warfare; after they passed, a mourning period of one year was customary. At that point, the tribe would notify neighboring tribes and ask for their help in selecting a new chief. The ensuing gathering was a major event for all tribal members involved.

Ceremony is a fundamental part of Passamaquoddy culture. Family groups traditionally gathered together for significant events, led by the appropriate chief of the village. Modern-era ceremonies recreate the experience and solidify the connection between the past and present. Here, a visiting chief walks along two lines of youths before reaching the hosting chief. On the right in the back is a small dog, traditionally a valuable ally to the Passamaquoddy.

The traditional dress of the Passamaquoddy consisted of a breechcloth, or loincloth, made from tanned deerskin or other animal hide, and leggings for additional protection. Unlike the indigenous peoples of the Southwest, the Passamaquoddy did not wear face paint or a bonnet headdress. Instead, as Chief Lewey demonstrates in this photograph, headdresses consisted of a headband with feathers stuck into it.

Close relationships with every generation have long been a major component of Passamaquoddy life. Children were accustomed to helping out in nearly every aspect, including hunting and fishing, while downtime consisted of playing games involving kicking a ball or playing with indigenous toys. Elders were honored for their accumulated wisdom and cared for as they became unable to tend to their own needs. Stories and legends of the surrounding areas were passed on from elders to youth, preserving culture, language, and song. Tight family units easily expanded at gatherings to include relatives of all ages. The Passamaquoddy pictured here in the 1920s are striving to maintain connection to their rich heritage by embodying these traditions. Beyond their extended family groups, the Passamaquoddy are part of a powerful and long-standing alliance, the Wabanaki Confederacy. Other members of the confederacy include the Penobscot, Micmac, Maliseet, and the Abenaki, each of whom are closely related to the ancestral bloodlines of the Passamaquoddy.

Among the islands of the Skutik is this particular land mass located directly in the river's center. Viewed from a shore lined with birch trees, the island was used by the Passamaquoddy to store food during the winter where it was safe from land scavengers and predators. As soon as the river was passable in the early spring, or whenever necessary, the food was retrieved.

Seen here from above in the modern era, that island—later known as St. Croix Island—was the site of the first major contact between the Passamaquoddy and European settlers. A party of Frenchmen arrived in the summer of 1604 and established what they believed would be the first settlement of New France.

The French party, led by Pierre Dugua de Mons and assisted by now-famed explorer Samuel de Champlain, determined the island to be particularly favorable after they arrived. It was thought to be safe from potential attack by the Passamaquoddy—a fear that ultimately proved baseless—and situated in an ideal mild climate with ample access to food and freshwater supplies.

Pierre Dugua de Mons, shown here immortalized in bronze in the form of a life-sized statue now located at the St. Croix Island International Historic Site, was given the charter to settle the lands of North America between what would become Virginia and Manitoba, Canada, by King Henry IV. St. Croix Island, so named for the cross-shaped formation the riverbank created near it, was meant to be the beginning of New France. (Author's collection.)

A total of 79 men were recruited for the mission of establishing a settlement on St. Croix Island. In the first few months, they rapidly set about building the rudimentary village, including several dwellings, farms, a great hall, and a home for Dugua. Skills such as carpentry were invaluable to the task of building, resulting in the felling of nearly every tree on the island before winter arrived. (Author's collection.)

The Passamaquoddy people met the French settlers amicably, according to Champlain's journals, and the two groups reciprocated in their curiosity about one another. They freely traded in supplies, food, and hunting and gathering techniques, enabling the French to gain a rapid foothold in the entirely unfamiliar environment. While they could not easily understand each other, the lack of hostility was clear. (Author's collection.)

Unfortunately, the French arrived during a period of exceptional cooling, and the winter of 1604–1605 was abnormally harsh. With the first snow flying in October, they labored to prepare the island for the quickly encroaching cold weather. As the temperature descended and remained low, their cider froze solid, and the only foodstuff available was salted meat. Many were unable to muster the strength to gather fuel to melt snow, and they drank whatever foul water they could obtain. By spring, 35 men had died from scurvy, and 20 more were at death's door. A timely arrival of fresh venison brought over by Passamaquoddy as soon as the ice floes cleared the river saved the lives of those remaining. Despite the challenging conditions, St. Croix Island is believed to have hosted the first Catholic and Protestant Christmas services north of Virginia as well as publishing the first "newspaper," *Master William*. The settlement was later moved to Nova Scotia, where the French gained a lasting foothold. For the Passamaquoddy and the St. Croix Valley, the settlement represented the beginning of profound change.

Two

Early Development of Calais
Late 1700s–1860s

The French settlement on St. Croix Island heralded a steady arrival of European explorers and traders accessing the remote region via its abundant shoreline. Most came in search of opportunity, seeking to transform the natural wealth of the valley into personal fortunes.

The most heavily traded items between the Passamaquoddy and Europeans were pelts exchanged for copper goods. Hats made from beaver pelts became popular in the high society of Western Europe, and so the animal became heavily sought by natives and European trappers alike. Otters, minks, foxes, and martens were similarly hunted until each species became scarce by the mid-1800s.

The population of Passamaquoddy faced a similar fate as foreign diseases and conflict ravaged the tribe. Approximately 90 percent of the native population perished by 1700.

It was lumber that drew the ambitions of the first permanent settlers of European descent in the region. Rugged men with a willingness to tolerate the wild frontier saw great potential in the immense forests filled with 150-foot white pines. In 1782, the first sawmill was built on the St. Croix River, signaling the beginning of an industry that fueled the growth both of what would soon become Calais and the newly independent United States.

Upon first being incorporated in 1809, Calais was part of what was then Massachusetts. The state held significant power from its capital of Boston, long a strong foothold of educated lawmakers. When the British launched the War of 1812 in an effort to reclaim their rebellious colony, the district that would become Maine was targeted in part for its shipping capabilities. In 1814, it was invaded by the British, and Eastport—located less than 30 miles from Calais near the mouth of the St. Croix—became the first American territory held by a foreign nation. The British remained in Eastport until 1818. The lack of protection offered by Massachusetts prompted a strong push for statehood, and in 1820, Maine became a state.

Shortly afterward, Calais grew rapidly in size, gradually overtaking all others in Washington County. By 1850, it was the largest city east of centrally located Bangor, the logging capital of the Eastern Seaboard.

During the height of the lumber industry, thousands of men from Calais and neighboring communities left for remote logging camps each fall. Once felled—typically by two-person crosscut saws measuring six feet in length—the giant pines and softwood trees were left where they lay. As soon as the ground hardened enough, teams of oxen or horses were sent in to retrieve them, depositing them on the iced-over river.

In the spring, the river melted, releasing the logs into waters rapidly flowing downstream where they would be gathered into booms and converted into boards by hydro-powered sawmills. Occasionally the logs would cluster together into a logjam, requiring river-drivers such as these to carefully navigate across them from the shore until they could be loosened with long hooks. The work was the most dangerous available in the state at the time.

Among the mills located on the St. Croix River was the one owned by James Murchie, born across the river from Calais in St. Stephen, New Brunswick, Canada. Murchie started his lumber venture in the 1850s and soon became one of the most industrious and well-known lumber barons in the region. These logs, having recently floated downstream, are ready for processing.

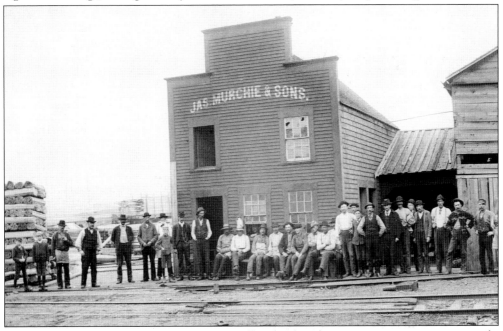

James Murchie did not make his fortune from selling lumber alone. He came to own seven vessels, six of which were large schooners, to transport his goods. He was also one of three proprietors offering full shipbuilding services, which his crew is prepared to render in this photograph. Other services available here included sail rigging and blacksmithing.

With the demand for quality boards from cities like Boston steadily increasing, the lumber industry in Calais flourished. In 1860 alone, 200 million board feet were shipped from the dozens of piers lining the St. Croix River, as shown in the 1856 map. The Calais wharfs—visible jutting from the left side of the shore, with St. Stephen, Canada, on the right—belong to the Murchies, Eatons, Halls, Peaveys, Todds, and McAlisters, among others, representing some of the most industrious families of the time period. Some of the lumber was used locally to meet the high demand for houses and buildings in the rapidly growing city, which reached a population of 5,621 by 1860.

Boards cut at the sawmills were transported to the docks along the Calais Railway, which, in 1838, became the first industrial railroad completed in the state of Maine. The railroad originally spanned a length of two miles, beginning at Salmon Falls upriver. Initially, carts were pulled down the tracks by horses, reducing their workload compared to pulling the log-laden carts up and down the hilly streets. In 1852, the railroad was lengthened to Baring, and in 1857, it was lengthened again to Princeton. By the late 1860s, wood-fired locomotives such as the G.M. *Porter*, shown here, provided a dramatic scene as they made their way along the tracks carrying 50,000 feet of lumber. This particular locomotive, which may have also been known as the *Princeton*, was the first to make the journey. The railroad was limited primarily to transporting cargo and played a major role in the St. Croix Valley's ability to ship lumber.

Early Main Street—shown here in the 1860s—was a constantly bustling place. Pedestrians walked alongside horses bearing riders and pulling carts through muddy streets, while sidewalks fashioned from wood and stone provided slightly easier walking conditions. Scores of wooden shops were erected by industrious businessmen selling everything from wares for ships, drugs, and

shoes to axes and woodstoves to combat the always-approaching winter. Work for carpenters in the area was steady, with 37 men listed as carpenters by trade in the local directory in 1850. By around 1860, a total of 221 vessels, some of them capable of carrying more than 1,000 tons, had been built in Calais itself.

The first church built in Calais was the Congregational church, seen here at right. The Congregationalists built the two-towered church in 1826 on Calais Avenue. The last service held in that location was in 1872, at which point the building was sold to James Pike and moved to Church Street, where it is pictured. It was known then as Pike's Opera House and sometimes used as the city building.

The year 1834 saw the erection of the city's second-oldest church, built by the Unitarian Society. In 1870, the Universalists across the river in St. Stephen joined the congregation, and thus it became the Union Church. Later, it was claimed by the Methodists and called Knight Memorial Methodist Church. The church stood tall at the foot of Calais Avenue until being torn down in 2015.

The First Baptist Church was built in 1934 in Milltown, an area located upriver that is now considered part of Calais proper. Fifty members of that congregation created the Second Baptist Church, shown here, in 1844. Sold to the Methodists in 1856, the church building was located on Main Street opposite Monroe Street's outlet before burning in 1882.

By 1853, it was widely recognized that Calais was in need of a town clock to unify the schedules of residents and sound an alarm as needed. St. Anne's Episcopal Church, built in 1853, fulfilled both needs with its massive clocktower located in the center of town on Church Street. Rev. G.W. Durell was the first rector and was instrumental in the building's creation.

In this view from the early 1870s, one can clearly see up Church Street from near its intersection with Main Street. On the left is the corner of the former Congregational church, then known as Pike's Opera House; on the right beyond the parked coach is the wooden Second Baptist Church (constructed in 1857, burned in 1882, and rebuilt in brick in 1885). Above that on the right is the clock tower of St. Anne's Episcopal Church, visible from nearly all points in town; inside is a large bell perfect for summoning citizens to service. A notable absence from the street is the grammar school that would be built at its apex in 1875. The sidewalks along the right are wooden, fashioned from the remains of the burgeoning leather tanning industry located upriver. The tannin in the bark of hemlocks was utilized in the tanning process to create a dark, rich red color, leaving the wood itself as "waste" by-product for use as sidewalks and similar purposes.

This building was among the first hotels in Calais; it was constructed in 1829 by John Barnard and known as Barnard's Inn. Beginning in 1836, it was the Frontier Hotel, operated by proprietors Mr. Ruggles and Mr. Hath. Later, it maintained the name St. Croix Exchange for a time, with the name simplified to the St. Croix Hotel in the modern era. It was torn down in 1983.

The largest hotel in Calais was the Temperance House, built in 1835 at the request of incorporators Samuel Kelley, Samuel Barker, and George Gavin. A three-and-a-half-story, nine-bay building with 42 rooms, this structure was the only brick hotel east of Bangor. It was later renamed the American House. In 1918, it was purchased by the St. Croix Masonic Association, under which it continues to serve as a meeting hall today.

One of the most influential businesses to lay claim to Calais was that established by John G. Beckett, a Scottish immigrant who made his way to the area in the 1840s. The son of a confectioner, he learned the trade and brought it to Calais in 1851. For the next century, the Beckett name was associated with highly favored delicacies such as honey sticks.

Fourth of July, 1858

Mr. J. G. Beckett is making great preparations for regaling the public on that day. He is making into confectionery no less than five barrels of sugar; he is also making into pastry, cake, pies, etc., as many as ten barrels of flour. And to wash it down he has any quantity of ginger, root, and hop beer, and cold soda. To keep cool he has any quantity of ice cream. It takes J. G. Beckett to do things up in shape —give him a call, one and all!

In this advertisement touting the upcoming July 4, 1858, celebration, the impact that the Beckett family has already had on the local populace's palate is evident. The community was undoubtedly looking forward to sampling ice cream, sodas—invented just a few decades prior in 1819—and an abundant selection of sweets.

The Civil War drew many Calais sons to the frontlines. While many travelled thousands of miles to fight, the most northern assault by the Confederates took place in Calais at the Bank of Nova Scotia in 1864. The robbery was thwarted by the loose lips of the attackers, who were awaited by an ambush of local militia—one of whom shot themselves in the foot in the excitement.

As one enters Calais from downriver, one of the first business sections to be met came to be known as "Carriage Row" for the way that it offered services and goods related to the transportation industry. In 1869, one such establishment was erected: M. Cone's Livery Stables. The tradition of transportation businesses in the location endures today, with Roger's Auto now occupying this spot.

A major shift in the mobility of the population came to Calais on 1824, when 200 people arrived on the steamer *New York* from Eastport. Within the next few years, steam-powered ships were making regular trips up and down the St. Croix and well beyond, including down the East Coast. The particular vessel seen here is the *Charles Houghton*, which began its regular operation in Calais in the early 1870s.

Three

THE BOOMING ERA
1870s–1890s

Immediately following the flooding and wind-borne devastation of the Great Saxby Gale of 1869—a storm that is estimated to have been equivalent to a modern Category 2 hurricane—Calais was faced with the greatest single disaster in its history. On August 27, 1870, a fire swept through Main Street, destroying dozens of buildings and docked ships. Its effect transformed the city into the brick-based downtown it remains today.

The residents of Calais, many of whom were now European immigrants, rallied, and from its ashes, industry and commercialism were swiftly restored. Brick buildings hosting numerous businesses came to dominate the streets, drawing businessmen from far and wide to the river city. The gradually declining lumber trade, which had decreased to 61 million board feet shipped in 1875 from 100 million just four years prior, was taking a back seat to Calais's emerging status as a mercantile hub.

The population of the city continued to increase, rising by 1,340 between 1870 and 1890 to now include 7,290 residents. The combined valuation of the residences of Calais reached $1,732,056 in 1880. By this time period, various houses of worship were well-established in Calais, along with 17 public schoolhouses instructing the area youth.

By all accounts, Calais was booming. "There are few Cities in Maine which have more reason to hope for a prosperous future than Calais," declared the *Calais Advertiser* in its September 28, 1881, issue.

To meet the needs of the growing community, a state-of-the-art electric streetcar system was built in the mid-1890s. As a result, residents of both Calais and St. Stephen could travel inexpensively along its seven-mile track, thus fully unifying the two cities and further dissolving the border between the United States and Canada.

Down the river, the discovery of exceptional red granite quarries launched a new industry, and a sub-village called Red Beach was formed. Red Beach, now recognized as part of Calais, was home to a world-renowned granite polishing factory and a plaster mill, in addition to hundreds of residents who found its location to be ideal.

As it prepared to enter a new century during a time of rapid technological change, Calais continued to evolve.

The infamous Great Fire of 1870 began behind a wooden building then owned by J.G. Beckett in a pile of straw. From that spark, 40–50 acres of downtown Calais were consumed in the blaze, including 79 homes and 13 vessels. Weeks of dry weather and a steady wind propelled the fire, which was not stopped even as efforts to blow up buildings in its path were employed.

In prior decades, Calais utilized a variety of firefighting tools, including this hand pumper designed in the 1820s. By 1863, it had three engines and five hose carts. There were two companies totaling 110 men—a force that still proved inadequate to the rapidly moving fire that saw business losses of more than half a million dollars, or $10 million in 2019 currency.

After the disastrous Great Fire of 1870, the Calais Fire Department built St. Croix No. 1 Firehouse in 1874, pictured at right. The new building integrated places to store modernized equipment, provided lodging for on-call fireman, and soon had a network of alarm systems installed between it and the homes of off-duty firefighters to quickly summon them.

Among the innovations developed at the St. Croix No. 1 Firehouse following the great fire was this system enabling horses to be easily rigged to engines and water tanks alike. As the horse enters in this photograph, the firefighting gent behind demonstrates the rapidity of response enabled by the hall's firepole.

A modern fire engine, on display in this photograph from 1875, is pulled by a horse no doubt harnessed by the previously pictured system. The company of firefighters is walking by Ganong's chocolate factory in St. Stephen. Firemen's musters between Calais and St. Stephen have a long tradition in the St. Croix Valley.

Calls to defend Calais from sudden blazes were frequent in the early days, and the Calais Fire Department was quick to respond and prevent any further fires on the order of the 1870 disaster. Here, it is successfully squelching a blaze that took hold of the upper levels of the St. Croix Exchange hotel in 1897.

Built between 1889 and 1896, the imposing figure that came to be known as Bank Corner was established at the intersection of Main and North Streets. As the colloquial name indicates, the building housed various banks over time, including Calais National Bank and Merrill Bank. Bank Corner stands tall today.

Main Street thrived in the decades following the Great Fire of 1870, as evidenced by this view down Main Street from the corner of North Street (Bank Corner being just behind the photographer). On the right is the Hill Brick Block, built in 1847; in 1890, it housed O.P. Treat's bookstore and Dr. Thomson's sarsaparilla laboratory. The Hill Brick Block remains as a Calais fixture.

Located at the bottom of Church Street, this area of Main Street was regarded as the center of town. At the time of the photograph, it was occupied by the Hill-Pike store, providing customers with a variety of groceries and wholesale goods by the barrelful. The Hill-Pike store was one of the busiest establishments in Calais.

Hunting and trapping continued to be a popular industry and sport in the region throughout this time period, as populations of native animals continued to persist. J.H. McMann's Variety Store is shown here, albeit slightly later in 1912, with no less than 141 bear skins displayed. The bear skins were sold to the London market.

Coal was a critical fuel for the St. Croix Valley in the 19th and early 20th centuries. Along with powering steamships and locomotives, both vital for industry and public transportation, coal was widely used to heat homes in specialized stoves. Accordingly, shipments of coal came in large quantities on three- and four-masted schooners to the wharf behind the train station.

Built in 1882 through the financing of Lewis Dexter, of Providence, Rhode Island, the cotton mill of Milltown, New Brunswick, employed hundreds of men and women—many from Calais—as spinners, weavers, and loom fixers. They were summarily added to the long list of Mainers working in the textile industry at the time. The $400,000 mill hosted 20,000 spindles running for most of the day, making it the largest in the world.

The logging industry maintained a presence throughout this time period, with logs visible along the upper portions of the frozen St. Croix River during the winter season. Horse-drawn sleigh rides down the river were an enjoyable pastime, provided one avoided the thinner spots of ice. Each year, the river reliably claimed one fatality through one misstep or another.

Among the fine hotels Calais was known for was the Emmans, once called Border City. It had 44 rooms and a dining hall large enough to host 100 guests. It was nearly always full on weekends, particularly throughout Prohibition, when the lax border ensured drinks were always plentiful for the thirsty traveler.

Originally the Ephraim Gates House—reputed to be the first hotel in Calais with running water—this c. 1865 building became known as the Sprague and later the Arcadian, Mecca, and Portside. An advertisement from the Arcadian in 1914 touts the availability of a clairvoyant palmist for 50¢ a reading. Whatever name it bore, the hotel was a steady hotspot throughout its life.

As much industry took place on the river, it was also a popular spot for recreation for Calais residents of all ages. These Victorian-era women are enjoying a dip—in full covering so as to not betray their modesty—as a three-masted schooner passes behind them. The distant shore is New Brunswick, Canada.

The busy city and its characteristically hardworking residents occasionally took time to enjoy parades, either as participants or spectators. Sometimes, as in this case, among those honored were the elders of the community, here riding in a cart pulled by magnificent oxen. Cattle were much more common work animals than horses, with some of the largest in the world, weighing more than two tons, raised in Maine.

The long winters afforded plenty of time for indoor activities such as playing the most fashionable board games of the day. These gents are enjoying their game of Crokinole, a dexterity-based game first developed in Ontario, Canada, in the 1870s bearing similarities to miniaturized curling. They are sitting in the Mason House, regarded as one of the finer residences at the time.

One of the first bicycles in Calais, variously called velocipedes or simply "wheels," belonged to Frank Moore, pictured at right as he and a friend pass the Border City (later the Emmans) Hotel. Moore's friend is driving an earlier "high-wheeler" model with a larger front wheel, a design that was particularly dangerous if the driver struck even a pebble. Moore's is the "safety" high-wheeler model designed in 1882.

Calais me

The citizens of Calais were well entertained during this time period at the Calais Opera House, an establishment known widely for staging exceptional plays and operas. Built in 1872, not long after the Great Fire of 1870, the Calais Opera House attracted such acts as the Boston Opera Company and the Eastport Opera Company, among many others. The longest-running play with the continually best attendance was *Uncle Tom's Cabin*, while the Gilbert and Sullivan comic opera *H.M.S. Pinafore* was equally beloved, to the extent that its words could be heard sung throughout town. Vaudeville acts at the opera house included unusual singers, magicians, acrobats, jugglers, and masters of trick bicycling; occasionally, trained horses filled the stage with their feats. Graduations from the Calais Academy, which hosted its own fine plays and musicals put on by the learned teachers and students, all took place at the Calais Opera House. The building remains standing today.

The post office was located in the Calais Opera House, and mail was dispensed, at least at one time, by this gentleman. The handwritten sign beside his window alerts the incoming resident that the mail has been delayed by three hours. Mail service, which came by steamship and by rail, was sometimes tenuous, particularly in the winter months. It was delivered to homes by wagon.

Built in 1892, the Calais Free Library enabled unprecedented access to the noteworthy, popular, and rare books of the day to the public of Calais at no cost. Previously, the city operated a subscription-based library with a collection that suffered significant damage in the great fire. James Shepherd Pike donated the land on which the library was built.

The First Congregational Church, still standing on Calais Avenue, was completed in 1873. At the time, the invocation was performed by the Reverend Dr. S.H. Dexter, of Calais, and the dedicatory prayer was given by the former pastor, the Reverend Dr. H.V. Keeler. Dr. Charles Swan, among the first medical doctors in Calais, directed the music.

CATHOLIC CHURCH AND CONVENT, CALAIS, ME.

The Catholic faith has held a steady presence in Calais since the town's beginning. This scene near the intersection of Calais Avenue and Washington Street shows the school and convent on the left, built in 1885; the parsonage in the center; and the Church of the Immaculate Conception, completed in 1894, on the right.

Before the arrival of the automobile, train travel was the swiftest way to get inland, and the Calais Railway Station—built in 1898 adjacent to the city's original industrial tracks—provided reliable access to Bangor in a half-day's trip by the following year. The more ambitious railway traveler could reach Boston in 14 hours.

Public transportation around Calais could be found in the form of this horse-drawn taxi, seen here heading up North Street. This particular taxi covered the Milltown loop, transporting workers and shoppers between the downtown and the industrial and residential districts. Behind it, artist and photographer studios are housed alongside offices of dentists and lawyers.

The St. Croix Valley hit a fully modern stride when, in 1894, its residents began constructing the tracks for an electric streetcar system. By 1895, residents could travel between Calais; Milltown; St. Stephen, New Brunswick; and Milltown, New Brunswick, for 5¢. Subsequently, the St. Croix Streetcar was one of four in the United States to ever cross international borders.

The streetcar service was opened in Calais on July 1, 1894, an event attended by thousands from both sides of the river. Initially, even though the tracks were laid and the electric system was ready in St. Stephen, the streetcar could only run through Calais—a situation that was remedied when the old wooden bridge connecting the cities was replaced by a modern steel construct in 1895.

One of the most well-known scenic streets is Calais Avenue, viewed here from where it meets Main Street. The early incarnation was lined with elm trees, making it a popular destination for travelers seeking shade. Dutch elm disease devastated the species in the 20th century, making maple one of the more common trees today. At left, the edge of the Temperance (American) House is visible.

Prohibition was strictly adhered to by some in Calais—and less so by others—periodically through the Victorian era. Either way, upright establishments such as Beckett's offered a selection of alternative beverages they touted as "Temperance Drinks." This advertisement from 1895 includes birch, Peruvian, Mexican sherbet, and pine apple, along with the notice: "For family use, the orange phosphate and ginger ale are unsurpassed."

In the 1870s, red granite of the finest quality was identified down the river in Red Beach. Quarries were quickly established around the community to mine the rock. Skilled laborers with the Maine Red Granite Company, founded in 1875, earned $1.75 for putting in a 10-hour day. Their unskilled coworkers made $1.15 for the often brutal work.

The quarried granite was transported in massive slabs on stone sleds pulled by either oxen or horses to the polishing factory shown here. Reportedly the best polishing plant in New England at the time, the factory included a number of polishers and column cutter machines, along with a McDonald stone-cutting machine.

The wharf in Red Beach enabled the steady flow of quarried granite and plaster materials to and from points far and wide. Red Beach granite was utilized in the Museum of Natural History of New York; the plant cases around terraces in Washington, DC; and in various courthouses and churches across the country.

In 1893, the fundraising efforts of the Ladies Memorial Society of Calais were made manifest in the form of the Soldier's Monument in Memorial Park. The handsome statue honored those lost in the Civil War and bears the inscription: "The soil out of which such men are made is good to be born on, good to live on, good to die for, and good to be buried in."

Just a few years after the Soldier's Monument was raised, the sons of Calais were once again called to battle, this time in the Spanish-American War of 1898. Here, Company K is marching towards the upper wharf in Calais as townsfolk of all ages line the streets to see them off.

Company K of the 1st Maine mustered in the state capital of Augusta and, with 979 men and 46 officers, departed from Calais in part on the steamer *Rose Standish*. After spending three months in Georgia, the company was not deployed further, and it was shortly mustered out by December 1898, having thankfully seen no combat.

Four

A THRIVING 20TH-CENTURY CITY
1900s–1910s

The turn of the 20th century saw Calais at the peak of its prosperity. With an electric streetcar system running through its major corridor and joining it to neighboring St. Stephen, a railway linking it to the rest of the state and beyond, and steamships running regularly, the residents of Calais enjoyed unparalleled mobility. Fine hotels and eating establishments lined the downtown streets, while purveyors of domestic and exotic goods enjoyed a steady business from shoppers who traveled many miles to reach the commercial center of the county.

Accordingly, the population of Calais reached its peak during this time period. The 1900 census recorded 7,655 residents, while some estimates in the few years following reported closer to 8,000 living in the bustling city.

For the Passamaquoddy, the situation was entirely different. In the previous decades, the federal and state governments began employing forced assimilation practices that removed children from their homes and sent them to boarding schools that would later be revealed to be rife with systemic abuse. The loss of land and the ability to utilize traditional hunting methods further jeopardized the tribe. In 1906, a total of 14 births were recorded for the Passamaquoddy, with 18 deaths in the same year.

Calais itself rounded the corner of prosperity before reaching its centennial anniversary in 1909. By the next year, the population declined to 6,116. The dramatic difference—a 20 percent decrease in a decade—foretold the trend of the following century.

At the time, however, residents viewed their city as among the most advanced, scenic, and fortunate of the Northeast. Within a decade of the century's turn, Calais saw its first personal vehicle on the streets, while just up the river in Baileyville, the largest paper mill in eastern Maine was constructed.

As quickly as technology was changing the face of Calais, so, too, was social change in the air. The educated women that filled the city were staunch supporters of the suffrage movement, expressing as such in large numbers in the 1917 elections. Two years later, the state passed their right to vote.

As the new century dawned, one of the first places its light reached was Calais—and not just because of its easterly location. This view of Main Street shows the streetcar in full swing transporting residents and visitors alike to their pleasure or their business. On the left is the edge of the Hill-Pike store, still busy providing groceries and provisions to the community. On the right is the Calais Opera House, which continued to serve as the post office for much of the century's first decade. The edifice of the Union Church at the corner of Calais Avenue can be seen at right, looming large over those entering downtown from the direction of Red Beach, Robbinston, Perry, Pleasant Point, and Eastport. Horse-drawn carriages were still the dominant mode of personal transportation for townsfolk, but that situation would rapidly be changing.

In 1904, the first arrival of the horseless carriages proved to be exciting news around the St. Croix Valley. It came in the form of a 1903 Stevens-Duyea, an electric vehicle with a top speed of 10 miles per hour. It was owned by a Mr. Curren, listed as a manager of the streetcar system. A year later, Dr. Charles Murphy brought the gasoline-powered specimen at right to the valley.

The news of the day was covered in part by the *Calais Advertiser*, a weekly newspaper founded in 1836 by John Jackson, who would serve as its editor for several decades thereafter. By 1900, the business of rapidly producing papers was transformed with the introduction of the linotype machine, used here by John Petit (right).

By far the biggest news of the valley was the construction of a massive paper mill and associated dam up the river in Baileyville. It was completed in 1905 entirely through the labor of 1,000 Italian immigrants. By the following year, 300 people were employed in producing 90 tons of paper each day.

In Milltown, located just up the river from Calais proper, workers and residents would have often visited S.S. Pineo's store on Main Street. Pineo was well-known as Milltown's most prominent merchant for several years. Among the goods sold at S.S. Pineo were Old Honesty Flour and the locally famous Dr. Thomson's Sarsaparilla, a tonic produced in Calais that promises it "cures where others fail."

This scene, captured in the first decade of the 20th century, touches on several stories relevant to the time period. In the foreground is the groundwork of what will become the new Calais Post Office. On the left is an unusual building style not commonly seen in New England: a minaret. It was built at the request of clothier Bruno Kalish, whose family hailed from near the eastern end of the Mediterranean Sea. The minaret was built as a comfort to Kalish's father, to remind him of the land he left when he came to Calais. Right of center is a wooden structure known as the Kalish Building; it housed the Kalish family for many years. One of the Beckett & Co. stores is located left of center, completing the picture of Calais's downtown being shaped in large part by immigrants.

Baptist Ch. Calais Hospital Court House Fire Station
by H. F. Lamb Historian & Photog

The Kalish story continues with the construction of the new City Building in 1901. When Bruno Kalish was elected mayor, he determined that the city needed a proper City Building. As he also owned a brickyard, he proposed brick for its construction and is said to have turned a tidy sale as a result. The building was constructed, and the incident was but one of many that colored Kalish's time as mayor.

Post Office, Calais, Me.

After several years of construction, the Calais Post Office was completed in 1909 to great fanfare. Built from white marble, the building literally gleamed in the heart of downtown Calais, and it was long the pride of the residents who made frequent use of it. Its large back windows provided an exceptional view of the St. Croix River.

While downtown Calais offered some of the finest hotels in Washington County, their rates were not affordable to everyone. The Boundary House in Milltown, located near a bridge going directly to Canada, doubtless attracted a large variety of those valuing the principle of free trade above all else. In 1901, rooms were $1 a day—less than $30 in 2019 currency. The proprietor at the time was F.W. Hinckley.

On the opposite end of the spectrum was DeMonts, a retreat hotel for wealthy residents looking for a night away from the city. Located at Devil's Head, just down the river from St. Croix Island, Hotel DeMonts was built in 1890 by ambitious entrepreneurs who were no doubt disappointed when it burned down less than two decades later.

Some establishments offering lodging aimed to attract a particular crowd. Among them was the Andrews Hotel, located on Main Street near the newly constructed steel bridge at Ferry Point. Completed in 1900, the hotel sold itself as being "dry," meaning travelers would have no luck finding alcoholic beverages to drink on premises. Later, it became Andrews Tobacco store.

DeMonts was occasionally the site of large celebrations in its short lifespan. One of the ones held on its pier was this 1904 commemoration of the tercentennial anniversary of the arrival of the French on St. Croix Island. The event was attended by thousands from both sides of the border who celebrated on both land and sea.

Regarded as the largest celebration to have occurred in Calais, the 1909 centennial event attracted 20,000 people to the St. Croix Valley. The day included a massive parade, games and activities for children, and the dedication of a black granite fountain in Memorial Park. Gov. Bert M. Fernald and Mayor W.J. Fowler led the proceedings. "The welfare and prosperity of any community depends largely on the character and disposition of its citizens, and judging from what I knew of your people before and what I have seen and heard since I arrived, I can say without reservation that I believe Calais has been in the past, and is now, unusually fortunate in this respect," Governor Fernald began. The four-and-a-half-ton granite slab, shaped into an elegant fountain by O.S. Tarbox, was donated by Henry B. Eaton, of the Eaton lumber barons.

Among the immigrants to call Calais home was Luigi Bernardini, formerly of Italy. The enterprising Bernardini rented a small shop on Main Street at the age of 19 or 20, sleeping in the back with his American wife. As his successes mounted, he purchased the shop's building, then the rest of the block. The Bernardinis opened the Boston Shoe Store soon after, shown here at the celebration of the 1909 centennial.

The centennial was recognized on buildings throughout the downtown, with the Calais Opera House joining in to don full patriotic plumage. In 1903, the first moving pictures were shown at the opera house, and by 1909, the motion picture industry was steadily working to put out silent films made using gradually improving technology.

The Passamaquoddy were regular participants in the celebrations that took place in Calais, though their purposes were rarely the same as those held by European descendants. Any available means were taken to preserve cultural heritage by the surviving members of the tribe, including showcasing traditional dress. Not far from where this float is passing, the first ethnographic field recordings in the world were made of Passamaquoddy wanting their culture to persist.

Since the 1700s, the Passamaquoddy were allotted two pieces of land to make their living on: one being the traditional summer village, Sipayik, and the other being the traditional winter village, Motahkomikuk. Referred to as Pleasant Point and Indian Township respectively, the reservations were home to scenes such as this one at Sipayik, where sealskins dry at Sabattis Lola's house.

Electric snow plow off track at Milltown, Maine.

As advanced as the electric streetcar system was, it was no match for the elements of the St. Croix Valley. The continual shifts between frosts and thaws eroded structures, contributing to the collapse of the bridge running over the railroad tracks by the Ferry Point Bridge. During the winter, keeping the rails free from ice was sometimes impossible, and even the plow sent to clear the snow would go off track and careen into the unfortunate surroundings (as it did here in Milltown). Occasionally, the streetcar stopped running for a simpler reason—such as when its power cord slipped out from the cable lining the tracks.

CALAIS HOSPITAL GALAIS ME 34

When accidents occurred, as they were wont to do in the era of poorly regulated technology or for any kind of malady, Calais residents and the extended community came to the hospital opened in 1917 by Dr. Walter Miner. Located on Church Street in a former Victorian residence, the hospital was much more convenient than Chipman Memorial Hospital in St. Stephen. Upon opening in January, the hospital employed four nurses as well as an orderly responsible for tidying the rooms. It would remain under Dr. Miner's management until 1939, when a group of local businessmen purchased it to maintain its operations. An annex for expecting mothers was established in the 1940s on Hinckley Hill. The main building of the hospital continued in this location until moving to Palmer Street in 1954. The former hospital was cleared to make room for the municipal parking lot at nearby city hall.

Class of 1906 in Washington

The mobility of young Calais residents had reached exciting new levels, and the 1906 graduating class of Calais Academy were no slouches in enjoying it. They took a class trip to Washington, DC. To reach this point, these classmates would have traveled 800 miles by rail—a distance few would have had any familiarity with. As automobiles had only come to Calais just a few years prior, the bus they are riding would have been another first.

The pinnacle of Church Street was crested by the Calais Grammar School once it was completed in 1875. Students from around the community hiked their way through the often frozen streets to receive an exceptional education through the eighth grade. Once finished, they moved next door to Calais Academy, where they would, with study, receive their high school diplomas.

With the earliest basketball court in North America said to be located in nearby St. Stephen, it is easy to imagine why Calais has had a long history as a basketball town. Shown is the 1905 high school team and its presumed mascot at the players' feet. Since the game first caught on, both genders of the Calais Blue Devils have claimed many state championships.

Along with basketball, football was a popular passion for the more physically aggressive youth and adults in the area. The 1903–1904 high school team is seen here wearing what amounted to minimal protection for the tackle sport. The adult league saw competitions with teams from around the county.

The third sport in Calais's trinity of athletic interests is baseball, which drew hundreds of spectators to the newly established fairgrounds and ballfield on Calais Avenue. The houses in the background line Lafayette Street. The ballfield remains an important component of the Calais community today in the form of the Thomas DiCenzo Athletic Complex.

Next to the ballfield was the Calais Fairgrounds, opened with great enthusiasm on July 4, 1911. The fairgrounds provided a place for entertainers and exhibitions of all kinds, including amusement rides, circuses, and a racing track that pitted trotters against one another at high speeds. Residents soon engaged in breeding trotters for the sport, until the fairgrounds stopped regular operations in 1917, aligning with the declaration of the United States' entry into World War I.

St. Croix Island was a popular picnicking and swimming spot for residents seeking a break from the heat on the mainland. Its sandy shores were ideal for the purpose, though it was soon recognized that they made the island particularly vulnerable to erosion. Franklin and Eleanor Roosevelt were among its frequent visitors.

The abundance of fish in the St. Croix River is literally the stuff of legend, with some tales describing the salmon runs as being so thick that one could walk across on their backs. Fishing was a popular pastime and a source of food for many in the Victorian era, including this group trying its luck from DeMonts pier.

An alternative to St. Croix Island was having a picnic on the rugged shoreline. This group, sporting the highest fashions of the day, has ventured downriver to find a suitable spot for its midday lunch, traveling by boat for convenience. Awaiting to tend to the group's needs are the hired hands watching from the anchored vessels.

The celebration in Calais that welcomed the soldiers returning from World War I filled the streets. Hundreds of men from the area left to fight in Europe, including many that joined the Canadian forces before the United States officially declared its entry into the fray. Two brothers, Fred and Harry Sherman, were among those that saw combat on the frontlines and did not return. The ensuing Calais American Legion, Sherman Brothers Post No. 3, is named in their honor.

Five

A TIME OF RAPID CHANGE
1920s–1950s

By the 1920s, Calais was beginning to show signs of struggle as its industries weakened. The last of the sawmills on the river slowed and then stopped, leaving the production of paper in Baileyville the lone remnant of the logging industry. Granite was less in demand as cement became increasingly inexpensive and easier to produce, leaving the quarries of Red Beach vast and quiet. The Great Flood of 1923 was itself instrumental in influencing local industry's collapse, as it devastated the cotton mill and virtually anything else located adjacent to the river.

Despite the steady blows to its prosperity, Calais continued to rally, and new industries, including shoemaking, clothing production, and sardine packing, employed hundreds of residents in factories of variable quality. The opening of each enterprise was met with enthusiasm, as making ends meet without a steady income became increasingly challenging during the Great Depression and the Second World War.

The sharply precipitous population drop between 1900 and 1910 to 6,116 residents was not repeated again, and when the census was taken in 1920, Calais had decreased by only 32 residents. The gradual decline continued in fits and starts, however, and in 1950, the city recorded a population of 4,589, hundreds of whom were part of the baby boom.

Within these four decades, Calais lost and erected new grammar and high school buildings, and a modern hospital was constructed. Civil societies such as the Calais Rotary Club and the Calais Lions Club enjoyed the energetic participation of the townspeople, many of whom saw the baby boom as evidence of resurgence. The drive to improve the community and the well-being of those in it was fully evidenced by both city administration and layfolk alike.

New businesses took root in the downtown area, including diners, movie theaters, and chain and retail stores. For the first time, growing families had the ability to easily purchase goods on store credit, signifying a shift in perspective and in lifestyle for those embracing the promise of the American Dream.

In the beginning of May 1923, the St. Croix River swelled to a size far greater than any had witnessed before. The flooding was the result of a dense, heavy snowpack accumulated over the previous winter and steady spring rains that fell relentlessly. With no other outlet, the water spilled over the riverbanks and into the homes of Milltowners and Calais residents alike. The damage was extensive enough that the *New York Times* reported on it. Four of the five functioning bridges connecting Calais and St. Stephen were swept away, leaving only the steel Ferry Point Bridge intact. The cotton mill, the largest employer of both Calais and St. Stephen residents, was completely flooded out, leaving its machinery in ruins. Once the pride of the St. Croix Valley for its modernity and its production capacity, the cotton mill remained quiet for years as the owners worked to raise money to repair it. The Eaton mill, shown here from the Canadian side of the river, was similarly demolished.

One of the most recognizable figures in Calais for decades was City Marshal Bobby Kerr, seen here in the 1930s at the corner of Monroe and Main Streets. Before becoming a marshal, Kerr was a streetcar operator from 1907 to 1919, at which point he joined the ranks of law enforcement. Kerr patrolled the streets for years before earning his promotion to police chief, a position from which he retired in 1953.

The regulation of the border and the people and goods crossing over Ferry Point Bridge is monitored by the US Customs office. In 1936, Customs received a major upgrade in the form of this modernized brick building. Beginning in 1924, the regulatory work of the customs agents was augmented by the efforts of the newly created US Border Patrol.

The governance of Calais is performed in part by the city council, elected officials serving two-year terms alongside the elected mayor. An appointed city manager handles the overall management of the city, with several department heads assisting him or her. In the 1930s, the council held its meetings on the upper floor of the City Building in a room that also served as the courthouse.

Good-natured jesting has long been a theme for city administrators. In 1928, Alderman Jim Rigley bet Mayor Ernest "Jack" Woodman that Al Smith would beat Herbert Hoover in the presidential election. After losing, a dummy representing Rigley was hanged in effigy in front of Goode Café. While in fun, the scene evokes the story of game poacher Calvin Graves being sentenced to hang in Calais in 1887—a sentence that was fortunately never carried out as the state overturned capital punishment soon after.

Ed Boyd, who served as both mayor and a member of the city council, was instrumental in connecting Calais with its namesake, Calais, France. The two cities exchanged gifts in 1935. Red granite from St. Croix Island was sent to France via the liner *Normandy* on its inaugural voyage. The gifts from France, including a chest, tapestries, and newspaper clippings, were displayed at the Calais Free Library.

Throughout its history, the Calais Free Library has enjoyed the service of many distinguished head librarians. From the 1930s to the 1940s, Emma Boyd, seen here, welcomed children and adults alike in their quest for knowledge and enrichment. She was succeeded by Edith Beckett, who worked with her previously as an assistant.

Past Presidents Calais Rotary Club   *Oct 29, 1941*   PHOTO BY W. Stracey Studios

Established in 1925, the Calais Rotary Club has long included some of the most prominent political and mercantile residents of Calais in its ranks. The club endeavors to raise funds for various causes in the city, including education and civic development, along with organizing events and activities to raise public engagement. Seen here in 1941, these Rotarians include Arthur Unobskey, Clarence Beckett, Cliff Chase, and Frank Beckett, each of whom played a major role in the growth and success of the early-20th-century community in Calais. The Rotary continues to operate in Calais with an ongoing close relationship to the St. Stephen branch that wholly fulfills the overall international mission of the global Rotary Club. Its modern ongoing initiatives include a Turkey-A-Thon, an annual fall fundraiser that provides turkeys to families in need across Washington County.

In 1954, construction began on a fully modern hospital with operatories and patient beds. The new building, located on Palmer Street, was the source of much excitement in the community while it was being erected. William Goode was the president of the hospital at the time. Those present in this photograph include Gov. Edmund Muskie and the Calais City Band, always a fixture at major community events.

The newly renamed Calais Regional Hospital opened its doors to patients on January 4, 1956, prompting a major effort by the nurses to transport their charges to the new facility. The building shown here had additions built onto it, some of which have since been destroyed, leaving the original structure intact. Calais Regional Hospital continues to operate as a critical access hospital.

Beckett and Company 100 Anniversary Rod and Gun Club 1951

The 100th anniversary of Beckett & Co.'s operations in Calais was celebrated in proper fashion with a massive field day open to past and present employees and their families. The day's events, which included various games such as the Rolling Pin Toss, were held at the Calais Rod and Gun Club, a place favored by armed outdoorsmen practicing their aim.

One of the oldest buildings still standing in Calais—the Holmes Cottage, built in the late 1700s or early 1800s—was restored in the 1950s through the efforts of resident Charles Livingstone and several civic-minded allies who banded together as the St. Croix Historical Society after the donation of the cottage and the nearby Holmestead from Josephine Moore. The building served as the first doctor's office in town for Dr. S.S. Whipple, Dr. Cyrus Hamlin, and Dr. Job Holmes.

At the top of Church Street runs Academy Street, so named for the presence of the building seen here on the right. The Calais Academy graduated hundreds of exceptional academics into the world since it was built in 1851. It burned in 1945. Next to it is the gymnasium, completed in 1923 and still standing today.

Originally built in 1875, the grammar school burned to the ground in 1935, and this brick building replaced it two years later. It remains intact as an apartment building to this day.

When fire destroyed Calais Academy in 1945, Calais was in financial distress and could not afford to build a new school unless it could declare the town a school district and request funds. Clarence B. Beckett, former mayor, advisor to the governor, and legislator, played a major role in getting the necessary credentials put forward, and a new school was constructed at the corner of Church Street and Washington Street. Said to be a state-of-the-art facility, the school had modern classrooms and a gymnasium integrated into it. The first class to graduate was that of 1948. It included familiar family names such as those born by Joan Beckett, Gladys and Lorraine Boyd, and Margaret Boardman, along with many other dynasties that had become part of the fabric of the community. Students received their secondary education at Calais Memorial High School until a new facility was constructed down the river. The last class to graduate from this particular building was in 1976.

In 1931, the public and esteemed officials gathered along the banks of the St. Croix by Devil's Head to witness the arrival of the new Pan Am Sikorsky S-40, an amphibious plane with four engines employed by the Commercial Transportation Company. The plane was en route from Boston to Halifax, Nova Scotia.

A decidedly less celebratory event took place on July 20, 1924. Bert Spinney, Tommy Hinds, Morris Hinds, William Thompson, and Vernald Powell were out for a drive in Spinney's Maxwell touring car. James Sullivan, of Lubec, collided with the group in his Hudson while speeding, leading to the loss of three lives and the name "Dead Man's Curve" being granted to the scene of the accident thereafter.

Despite the dangers and road-based challenges of the automobile, its popularity increased as Calais and St. Stephen residents embraced the independence of movement it granted them. The St. Croix Streetcar, with Car No. 4 seen here crossing Ferry Point Bridge, ran its last run in 1929 as the economic slowing of the Great Depression took root.

Opened in 1880 on the St. Croix River, the sardine factory Frontier Packing provided work for an increasing number of Calais residents as the industrial tide turned. The following year, a second factory, H. Wentworth and Company, increased the ranks of sardine packers in the community, with several more factories, including the Holmes one above, soon cropping up. In 1938, the production slowed, a trend that continued until the industry collapsed fully in the 1960s.

The production of shoes in Calais briefly occupied the community in large numbers around the turn of the 20th century. The Rowen Moore Shoe Factory, located at the bottom of Barker Street, provided employment for hundreds of people while it was in operation. The Trimble Shoe Factory, built in 1904, similarly had high production until it caught fire in 1914.

After shoe production in Calais dwindled in the 1930s, Ware Knitters moved into the former Rowen Moore building. A Massachusetts-based operation, Ware Knitters put hundreds of women to work to meet the need for military uniforms as World War II loomed large on the horizon.

By the 1950s, the former Rowen Moore building was known as Kobre's Woodworking, an operation that doubtless involved a significant amount of flammable materials. Eyewitnesses remembered hearing a series of explosions as the massive building was quickly engulfed by flames.

The Passamaquoddy continued to practice and pass on cultural traditions to their youth when possible. Frances Molly is shown here creating a fine sweetgrass basket with her daughter Josephine Tomah in Indian Township around 1922. Traditionally made for their utility, the baskets held increasing value as pieces of art.

Ralph Rife, manager of the J.C. Penney, lived with his wife, Marjorie, in a large home on the corner of Main and Barker Streets. The childless couple converted their home into the Wickachee Inn, offering lodging and later a dining room for their patrons. Rooms were available for $1 a person. The Wickachee remains a popular gathering spot today.

One of the most iconic buildings in Calais is the unassuming structure seen here. Located where one enters the downtown from St. Stephen, this building was claimed by Ed Williamson as a fish market in 1951, offering fine, fresh seafood to the city. Afterward, it gained famed as the Angelholm restaurant, owned by Swedish immigrant Ole Olsson. Today, it persists as Jo's Diner.

In 1925, one of the oldest veterans' groups in Calais, the Joel A. Haycock Post No. 34 of the Grand Army of the Republic, held its last memorial service. Consisting of the veterans of the Civil War, only five members remained to participate in the service when this photograph was taken.

While veterans may age, war does not. By 1941, the world was at war, even while the United States remained uncommitted. In Calais, dozens of men signed up to fight for the Canadian forces as they had in the past. The following year, Calais was identified as one of 19 places in Maine likely to be bombed, and air-raid shelters and observation towers were erected and continuously manned.

The official entry of the United States into the war following Pearl Harbor transformed the Calais community. Rationing quickly became standard, with sugar among the first items targeted. A complicated stamp system was utilized, limiting the purchase of many household goods to those who possessed them. When scrap was needed to fuel the war effort, Arthur Unobskey organized a very successful drive outside the railroad station.

The close of the 1950s was met with the last showing at the State Theater, a popular attraction amongst the youth of the valley since it opened in 1928. The week after this February 26, 1958, flyer was released to the papers, the theater caught fire while 300 moviegoers were enjoying these films. No one was hurt, but the theater never opened again.

Six

SLOWED MOMENTUM
1960s–1990s

With baby boomers filling the businesses and residences of Calais, the downtown area was a lively place in the opening of the second half of the 20th century. Nearly every household possessed an automobile—some of them several—and the streets were lined with models new and old as their owners dined and shopped in the large department stores and small shops that Main Street claimed.

So robust was the youth population at this time that 1966 saw the biggest class ever at Calais Memorial High School. A few years later, in 1969, Washington County Vocational Technical Institute opened as part of the state's effort to provide an alternative path to youth who were not interested in academia. The college was located down the river along the banks of the St. Croix on an old farm; it originally offered programs in home construction, boatbuilding, and wood harvesting. In 1977, a new high school was constructed adjacent to the college, creating a unified secondary and post-secondary campus that remains today.

The 1980s saw the fall of two long-standing structures in Calais: the St. Croix Exchange hotel and the white marble post office. Other historic downtown buildings began to clearly show their age after a century of weathering the elements without significant restoration, and they lay dormant and crumbling while life in the community continued around them.

In the early 1990s, retail giant Walmart set its sights on Maine for expansion, and a store in Calais was proposed not long after. Some were in favor of its arrival and the promise of employment and inexpensive goods that it offered, but others were fearful of the impact the major national chain would have on local businesses. Either way, a new Walmart was built on South Street in a location it continues operating from today.

From 4,223 at the start of the 1960s, the population continued downward, reaching 3,447 by the end of the millennium as generations of youth left Calais to find work in larger urban centers.

The retail era of the mid-20th century was dominated in part by 5 and 10¢ stores that originally launched with a range of merchandise available for nothing more than a nickel or a dime. Newberry's, seen here during its grand opening, was one such establishment in downtown Calais. The luncheonette counter drew steady business from children and adults alike for the several decades it operated.

Among the businesses that persisted throughout the latter 20th century is Johnson Hardware. Originally started in the early 1950s by Rocky and Andy Johnson, it soon opened in a larger downtown location, seen here in the 1960s. Offering a selection of hardware for virtually all needs related to house maintenance, Johnson Hardware's goods proved to be in constant demand.

In 1961, a massive festival was organized to celebrate the unique history of Calais and St. Stephen as twin communities separated by an international border. Called Frontier Week, the organizers put together a 100-page program filled with events, history, and advertisements from nearly all businesses on both sides of the river. Included in the program were congratulatory messages from Pres. John F. Kennedy and Canadian prime minister John Diefenbaker, to name only a few of the politicians who recognized the significance of the occasion. To oversee the nine days of proceedings, an election was held, with ballots sent to all residents as well as dignitaries around the world—even communist countries. Its winner, Bob Treworgy, was best known for operating Treworgy's drugstore on Main Street in a location that previously hosted druggists Percy Lord and Rexall Drugs. As the winner of what is believed to be the only international election held between the United States and Canada, Treworgy received a symbolic key to the St. Croix Valley.

Among those who attended the ceremonies of Frontier Week were Louis Robichaud, premier of New Brunswick, and John Reed, governor of Maine. The two leaders were tasked to compete in a baseball game, with Reed playing alongside his executive council and Robichaud playing with his cabinet. Keeping score were umpires John Volpe, governor of Massachusetts, and Robert Stanfield, premier of Nova Scotia.

Spectators were not limited to the performance of politicians playing baseball thanks to the arrival of legendary Boston Red Sox player Ted Williams, who gamely hit a single for each side. Fresh from retirement in 1960, Williams was easily among the more popular attractions to Calais when he was a featured contestant in a fishing derby.

For decades, residents used the banks of the St. Croix River as a dumping ground. Everything from household furniture such as beds, couches, and chairs to automobiles were brought to the river and either carried off—in part or in whole—or buried under accumulating layers of mud and sawdust. The pollution was noticeable and problematic, with the river rendered unusable for most recreational activities by the time of this 1969 photograph. The problem was not a modern one, as in 1867, the Report to the Commissioner of Maine records pollution as one of the top three challenges facing the fish population (the others being impassable dams and overfishing). A pollution treatment plant was established in this location. Up the river in Baileyville, the St. Croix Paper Company was acquired by Georgia-Pacific in 1963, and the paper giant continued its operations for several decades. Industrial pollution is an ongoing problem for the river, named among the most polluted in the country at the turn of the millennium. The recent removal of upriver dams is returning the flow of key fish species as efforts to restore it continue.

The year 1970 saw the launch and successful completion of a massive citywide cleanup event with the goal of beautifying the streets once more. These young girls are diligently working on Eaton Street with the banks of the St. Croix River in the distance behind them.

Various organizations, businesses, and individuals participated in the citywide cleanup of 1970, including these members of the National Guard. The National Guard has maintained a presence on Calais Avenue since opening a branch in the city in 1947. It now operates as Detachment 2 of the 1136th Transportation Company.

First launched in the United States in 1926 by a group of retailers with a direct link to their suppliers, IGA was a major presence in cities and towns across the country by mid-century. In Calais, the IGA began its operations as a neighborhood grocery store on Main Street. On March 4, 1959, a new IGA grocery store was constructed at the intersection of Church and Washington Streets. In the late 1970s, it was purchased by Eddie and Kathy Bell, who managed it as Bell's IGA, in part from its current home on North Street. It continues to operate today under Robert Craft and David Pike, both of whom first started working at the store as young adults when it was located in the building shown here.

In the 1950s, mass merchandise retailer W.T. Grants relocated its operations when the former Kramer Block, located near the marble post office, burned down. W.T. Grants owned the block at the time, and it took the opportunity to build the modern store shown here in 1972. The Kramer Block was home to the Palace Theater, another popular spot for those looking for entertainment of the motion picture variety. In 1975, W.T. Grants followed the demise of its namesake a few years after his passing, and the 1,200 stores located around the nation were summarily closed following the second-largest bankruptcy in American history in 1976. This structure was eventually torn down, leaving a parking lot where it once stood.

Brooks Pharmacy, also known as Brooks Drugs, provided a convenient place for residents to fulfill their medicinal needs. The Brooks chain was extremely prominent in New England in the 1980s and 1990s, abruptly terminating after the turn of the millennium after being purchased by competitor Rite Aid.

Originally built in 1900 as the Andrews Hotel—offering its lodgers a completely "dry" experience without the troublesome presence of alcohol—this building was in operation as Andrew's Tobacco by the 1970s. Many residents fondly remember the hot dogs cooked in peanut oil the Andrews Hotel once served. After closing its doors, this building was demolished in the 1980s.

By the 1960s, McDonald's restaurants were opening up around the country by the hundreds each year. Calais was not excluded from the steady expansion of the giant burger chain, and the building that once housed O.P. Treat's bookstore and Dr. Thomson's sarsaparilla factory was now used primarily for McDonald's advertisement.

Up North Street, a second commercial hub persisted in the modern era, providing a home for various service and retail businesses. Along with restaurants, gas stations, and banks, the North Street shopping center district, shown here in midwinter, would later become home to the IGA and Johnson's after their respective relocations.

In October 1976, the community watched with dismay from afar as smoke rose from St. Croix Island. The lighthouse and the associated keeper's home were fully destroyed by the blaze, effectively removing the last of the major man-made structures remaining on the island.

One of the more controversial demolitions of the modern era was that of the marble post office in 1985. The structure had long been considered a source of pride for Calais residents, who were accustomed to admiring its elegance; challenging this perspective were business developers who saw the opportunity for encouraging economic growth.

Seared in the memory of residents who were present in the area at the time is the fire that destroyed Johnson's hardware store in the downtown district. The fire took place in July 1996 and became a spectacle that attracted concerned community members from both sides of the border. The Calais Fire Department was joined by the St. Stephen Fire Department in combating the blaze, enacting one of the few mutual-aid agreements existing between international municipalities.

Filled with ups and downs, the second half of the 20th century was not without its challenges to residents who knew Calais in its heyday. Appropriately, however, one of the enduring traditions to remain is the descendant of Frontier Week: the International Homecoming Festival, celebrating the uniquely international nature of the St. Croix Valley at the beginning of every August.

Seven

CALAIS TODAY
2000s–2010s

With a population less than half of what it was a century ago, Calais has unmistakably changed from when it was the commercial hub of Washington County. The increasing modernization of production pulled more and more families to larger cities, leaving rurally located municipalities like Calais without a major source of employment.

The industries that survive are the ones that have long persisted, albeit in new forms: The mill in Baileyville, after closing for a few years, is going strong under the management of an international corporation; the Mingo family operates a cranberry business, a tree farm, and a wreath-making operation that ships around the country; and the Passamaquoddy are once again catching elvers in the St. Croix River, transforming the young eels into record-breaking profits via the Japanese market.

While electric streetcars may no longer travel along the corridor of Main Street, the streets of Calais have been modernized in the most dramatic sense with the recent installation of a fiber optic internet network. Developed in partnership with Baileyville as part of a joint push for economic development, the broadband utility is the first in the state to be operated by municipalities.

In an appropriate twist, the municipality that first saw an automobile in the form of an electric car in 1903 now has the means to support the return of such rechargeable vehicles. In 2019, an electric car charger was installed behind the Calais Free Library, not far from where horses were famously watered at Pike's Park.

Modernization continues to improve the lives of Calais residents who benefit from technologies that offer telecommunication capabilities, removing the challenge of distance for some necessities and vocations. For the first time, telecommuters are making the most of the inexpensive cost of living in Calais while simultaneously working jobs for employers around the world.

Though increasingly departed from the days of small independent neighborhood shops, Calais continues to be attractive to major retailers. Walmart expanded to a superstore, and Tractor Supply, Label Shopper and the Dollar Tree all opened their doors in the past few decades.

The downtown, meanwhile, has come under the care of a robust community group—the Calais Downtown Revitalization Coalition. It is among the many organizations in the municipality working to ensure a thriving future.

A schooner returned to the St. Croix River in the modern era as part of the city's bicentennial celebration in 2009. The *Sylvania Beal*, operated as a whale watching vessel by the Eastport Windjammers at the time, was brought in for an evening cruise that members of the St. Croix Historical Society remember as being cold and wet.

The extended community attended a re-creation of the first city meeting—originally occurring in 1809—during the bicentennial celebration. Members of the St. Croix Historical Society joined local players for the presentation, thus building a bridge to the past in Memorial Park.

A newly installed sign welcomes those traveling from the Ferry Point crossing with St. Stephen, New Brunswick, to downtown Calais. In the background on the left is the building once known as Ed Williams's fish market, which later became the Angelholm. Today, it operates a steady business as Jo's Diner, best known for its pizza, fish and chips, and commitment to providing refreshments at community activities. On the right, in a shopping center owned by the Unobskey family, is Marden's, located where Rich's department store previously offered retail products. Marden's is a Maine-based company associated with the state's former governor Paul LePage (2011–2019); it attracts shoppers from throughout the area with its salvage-based deals. Opposite the sign and out of sight is the recently constructed Dollar Tree, located near where Andrews Hotel/Andrews Tobacco once stood. (Author's collection.)

The former railroad station, once a hotspot for activity in the passenger and cargo transportation industry, was converted into the Downeast Heritage Museum at the turn of the millennium with a $6.6-million investment by developers who saw the high traffic at the border crossing to be indicative of potential visitors. After a disappointing opening, the building was sold to the Passamaquoddy, who now run it as the Wabanaki Cultural Center.

Reconstruction has been the name of the game for many of the downtown's brick buildings, including Bank Corner, seen here. The facades of several eroding brick structures were restored in part through the Maine Community Development Block Grant. Bank Corner, now vacant, recently hosted the gift shop Urban Moose and the Katahdin Coffee House. (Author's collection.)

Other buildings have been rehabilitated through private ventures, such as the Sarsaparilla building at the corner of North and Main Streets. Extensive repairs were required to save the collapsing roof, after which the original painting on the front, including Dr. Thomson's portrait, were restored as well. (Author's collection.)

While the downtown has its challenges in terms of condition, the spirit of the community remains robust. Every August, the International Homecoming Festival is celebrated by members from all over the community alongside those who travel thousands of miles annually for the event. Here, members of the US and Canadian Color Guards lead the parade on Main Street. (Author's collection.)

Every year, just before Veterans Day, the rich history of military participation in the community is honored by the students of the AP English class at Calais Middle High School from the gymnasium of the conjoined campus it shares with Washington County Community College. All of the veterans and their families in the area are invited to attend an event that includes a

slideshow featuring photographs of local service members around or during their time of active duty as well as a reading of *America's White Table*. Attendees are handed roses by students in recognition and thanks for their service. (Author's collection.)

Many of the churches in Calais continue to enjoy robust participation from their members, including Second Baptist Church, seen here. The congregation has gathered for this occasion to celebrate the restoration of the original bell the church utilized in 1883. The bell sat unused and sinking into the mud on private property following a fire in 2001 that destroyed the church. Congregation members Roy Curtis and "Grampie" Bill Gibson were instrumental in building the housing for the bell and fundraising for its restoration, respectively, an effort heartily commended by Pastor Matthew S. Burden and the church's various officials and senior members. The 1883 bell was built by the Clinton H. Meneely Bell Company, of Troy, New York; Curtis spent approximately two and a half years working to create a period-accurate frame. The Second Baptist Church offers regular gospel concerts for the community to attend at no cost. (Author's collection.)

Directly adjacent to the Second Baptist Church is the *Calais Advertiser*, operating from its most modern location on Church Street. Among the oldest still-operating weekly newspapers in the country with a founding date of 1836, the *Calais Advertiser* was under the helm of Scotsman and Calais city councilor Ferguson Calder until it was purchased in 2013 by a Canadian partnership with an interest in preserving community newspapers. The award-winning paper continues its mission of covering relevant news from around Calais and the extended communities of Baileyville, Robbinston, Perry, Alexander, Cooper, and Eastport, among others. In an effort to promote community engagement and interest in local news amongst the youth, the paper launched an effort in 2017 to get paperboys and papergirls back on the city streets, resulting in the successful return of neighborhood deliveries. (Author's collection.)

One of the primary topics covered by the *Calais Advertiser* in 2016 was the expansion of the Baileyville mill, founded in 1905. The company expanded the operations of Woodland Pulp by adding machines necessary for producing 120,000 metric tons of tissue paper in a move that continues to provide employment for the area. (Author's collection.)

In sharp contrast to the still-thriving mill are the remains of the Red Beach granite and granite polishing industry. Known colloquially as "The Archives," the spot that once supported the factory has been reclaimed by the woods following a fire in the early part of the 20th century. Red granite pillars—both polished and unpolished—are strewn throughout the woods along trails long abandoned by the oxen and workers that once plied them. (Author's collection.)

Back in Calais proper, students of Calais Elementary School are shown fire safety techniques and the capabilities of fire equipment at the Calais Fire Station, now located in a facility on North Street that also houses the police station and public works. Firefighters engage students every year in various drills in an effort to increase their familiarity with both safety personnel and best practices in the event of a fire. (Author's collection.)

Along with hosting children at the fire station for a visit with Santa at Christmas and Easter egg hunts, the Calais Fire/EMS Department puts on games every year for the Fourth of July at the Thomas DiCenzo Athletic Complex. The event, which includes several activities, is a favorite among local youth. (Author's collection.)

The chill of deep fall is countered each year in Calais by Scarecrow Fest, a monthlong series of activities culminating in a single day of fun at the end of October. Throughout the month, businesses and individuals are encouraged to decorate downtown streetlamps with scarecrows of their choosing, leading to a wide range of creative scenes that fill Main Street each year—and lead to confusion amongst drivers waiting for the scarecrows to cross the street. Events at the end of the month typically include a Witches Walk, casket race, chili tasting, cadaver toss, and a mummy race, seen here taking place in Triangle Park in front of the Calais Free Library. The event is sponsored by the Calais Downtown Revitalization Coalition, and it goes hand-in-hand with the frequently concurrent Black Magic Bash, organized by the Calais Lioness group at the Calais Motor Inn. (Author's collection.)

Up the river at Washington County Community College (WCCC), graduations for students completing two-year and certificate programs are held each May when the student body walks together to Calais Middle–High School's gymnasium. They are led by students chosen to carry the US flag, the Canadian flag, the State of Maine flag, and the Passamaquoddy flag; once inside, they are welcomed by Passamaquoddy drummers singing the "Honor Song." WCCC has expanded its offerings significantly since first launching in the late 1960s. Today, students can choose from 20 areas of study, including computer technology, criminal justice, electromechanical instrumentation technology, heating technology, entrepreneurship, phlebotomy, and heavy equipment operations. Certain programs are created and tailored to meet the needs of local businesses, including nurses for Calais Regional Hospital and pulp technicians for St. Croix Tissue. The college's commitment to student success and its growing online curriculum combine to frequently place it in the top 25 of community colleges in the country. (Author's collection.)

Every year, as part of the International Homecoming Festival, the St. Croix Historical Society conducts a well-attended Cemetery Tour. The tour comprises a performance by local community members greeting their guests in the roles of long-deceased Calais residents. The backgrounds of the featured residents are heavily researched to produce an accurate script to best enlighten and engage spectators. (Author's collection.)

The downtown itself possesses many visible links to the past, including this mural of the *Rose Standish* steamship painted in 2016 by nationally renowned mural artist Amy Bartlett Wright and called *Sail to Steam, Calais, Maine 1899.* Wright was hired by the managing volunteers of the Irene Chadbourne Ecumenical Food Pantry to paint the mural on their recently acquired building, now used for a thrift store that raises funds for the widely accessed pantry. (Author's collection.)

The continual beautification of the downtown, including the maintenance of dozens of flower pots and decorative lights, is but one of the ways the Calais Downtown Revitalization Coalition (CDRC) helps to attract visitors and the community to downtown Calais. One of the more engaging events held in previous years is the Chair Affair, part of the International Homecoming Festival in August. Custom-made Adirondack chairs are given to participating businesses from around the community, each of whom decorate their chairs with a design relevant to their industry or contemporary culture. The chairs are then auctioned off in a lively contest held in Triangle Park, once the site of the mercantile Flat Iron Block, long since demolished. Triangle Park provides the scene for yet another CDRC activity: Music on the Green. Every Tuesday evening throughout the summer months, local musicians from around the community play for a crowd that includes all ages. In the background, left of the tree, Dr. Thomson surveys the proceedings from his as-yet-unrestored portrait atop the Sarsaparilla building. (Author's collection.)

The oldest residence in Calais, the Holmes Cottage, is open as a museum in the summer by volunteers from the St. Croix Historical Society. Inside are various relics from the past, some of which came from the Holmes family, including Dr. Holmes's medical log book dating to the 1860s, and some of which was donated by the community. (Author's collection.)

Colin C. Whitlock's Mill Light is among the properties under the care of the St. Croix Historical Society, along with the Holmes Cottage and the Holmestead. The lighthouse was built in 1892 on the site of Whitlock's mill; Whitlock customarily hung a lantern in the tree to ward passing vessels from the dangerous sharp turn on the river. (Author's collection.)

From a dark past in which dancing by Passamaquoddy and natives across the land was banned by the federal government in 1890, today's tribal members are freely able to engage in their rich heritage. Cultural leaders such as Walter Sockabasin perform an invaluable service in passing on these traditions to Passamaquoddy youth. (Courtesy of Donald Soctomah.)

Along with traditional dances and songs, Passamaquoddy tribal members such as Molly Jeanette Parker, shown here with grandchildren Emma and Donald Soctomah Jr., pass on crafting techniques that have been utilized in the St. Croix Valley for thousands of years. The baskets are customarily woven with sweetgrass, giving them a smell unlike any in the world. (Courtesy of Donald Soctomah.)

While St. Croix Island remains off limits to the public as a result of its vulnerable and eroding condition, a site has been established by the National Park Service on the banks of the river alongside it. The site offers several exhibits that share the story of the French and the Passamaquoddy in 1604–1605, including a series of life-size bronze statues and informational displays that can be heard in English, French, and Passamaquoddy. In 2019, the site expanded its indoor exhibit to include replicas of the more than 700 petroglyphs originally carved by the Passamaquoddy around Machias Bay. Tribal historian Donald Soctomah is seen here describing the four petroglyphs he chose for the exhibit: two of *m'teoulin*, spiritual men and women of the tribe—one of whom holds an open palm to show they are unarmed and welcoming—and two of Champlain's ship, one of which has the Christian cross alongside it. (Author's collection.)

The women of the Passamaquoddy perform the Tutuwas, or Pine Needle, dance each year as part of the Indian Days festival held at Sipayik (Pleasant Point). The dance replicates the movement of a tuft of pine needles dancing on a drum. The public is openly invited to attend the early-August festival to observe and occasionally participate in the traditional dances, songs, and ceremonies of the tribe. (Author's collection.)

Continuing to watch the unfolding story of the St. Croix Valley is the persistent white-tailed deer population. Fawns, does, and occasionally bucks are seen frequently in the neighborhoods and nearby woods of the community, traveling freely and relatively without fear as residents widely stop to admire them. (Author's collection.)

INDEX

ABOUT THE ST. CROIX HISTORICAL SOCIETY

Based in Calais, the St. Croix Historical Society aims to preserve the rich history of the communities surrounding the St. Croix River. The society began in 1954 following the donation of the land and buildings that once belonged to Dr. Job Holmes by his niece Josephine Moore. The 1850 Italianate Holmestead now serves as the society headquarters, while the nearby Holmes Cottage is maintained as a museum. Monthly presentations are held at the Holmestead, sharing local history with the public at no cost. Donating members of the society receive a regularly published newsletter. Visit stcroixhistorical.com to read dozens of free articles about the history of the St. Croix Valley, see a listing of our publications, become a member, and more.

DISCOVER THOUSANDS OF LOCAL HISTORY BOOKS
FEATURING MILLIONS OF VINTAGE IMAGES

Arcadia Publishing, the leading local history publisher in the United States, is committed to making history accessible and meaningful through publishing books that celebrate and preserve the heritage of America's people and places.

Find more books like this at
www.arcadiapublishing.com

Search for your hometown history, your old stomping grounds, and even your favorite sports team.